Top Super Bowls

BY RYAN JAMES

A Stingray Book

SEAHORSE PUBLISHING

Teaching Tips for Caregivers and Teachers:

This Hi-Lo book features high-interest subject matter that will appeal to all readers in intermediate and middle school grades. It may be enjoyed by students reading at or above grade level as well as by those who are looking for age-appropriate themes matched with a less challenging reading level. Hi-Lo books are ideal for ELL readers, too.

Each book appeals to a striving reader's age and maturity level. Opportunities are provided for students to read words they already know while encountering a limited number of new, high-interest vocabulary words. With these supports in place, students will read more fluently while increasing reading comprehension. Use the following suggestions to help students grow as readers.

- Encourage the student to read independently at home.
- Encourage the student to practice reading aloud.
- Encourage activities that require reading.
- Establish a regular reading time.
- Have the student write questions about what they read.

Teaching Tips for Teachers:

Before Reading

- Ask, "What do I know about this topic?"
- Ask, "What do I want to learn about this topic?"

During Reading

- Ask, "What is the author trying to teach me?"
- Ask, "How is this like something I already know?"

After Reading

- Discuss how the text features (headings, index, etc.) help with understanding the topic.
- Ask, "What interesting or fun fact did you learn?"

TABLE OF CONTENTS

What Is the Super Bowl?

The Super Bowl is the championship game of the NFL (National Football League). It is played between the winner of the AFC (American Football Conference) and the winner of the NFC (National Football Conference).

The first Super Bowl took place on January 15, 1967, in Los Angeles Memorial Coliseum.

The Green Bay Packers won 35 to 10 over the Kansas City Chiefs.

FUN FACT: **The Super Bowl trophy is named after Vince Lombardi, the head coach of the Packers team that won the first Super Bowl.**

VINCE LOMBARDI
TROPHY
NFL
SUPER BOWL
AFC vs NFC
Stadium
SUPER BOWL

Super Bowl XXXVI

February 3, 2002

NEW ENGLAND PATRIOTS	20-17	ST. LOUIS RAMS

LOUISIANA SUPERDOME, NEW ORLEANS, LOUISIANA

Quarterback Kurt Warner led a Rams team that was called "the greatest show on **turf**."

The Patriots were **underdogs**, but their **offense** was led by a quarterback who would become a legend–Tom Brady.

Patriots cornerback Ty Law **intercepted** the ball and ran 47 yards (43 meters) into the end zone. Patriots kicker Adam Vinatieri made a 48-yard (44-meter) game-winning field goal.

MOST VALUABLE PLAYER:

TOM BRADY

Super Bowl XXIII

January 22, 1989

SAN FRANCISCO 49ers **20-16** CINCINNATI BENGALS

JOE ROBBIE STADIUM, MIAMI GARDENS, FLORIDA

After each team scored two field goals, the score was tied at 6 to 6.

Kick returner Stanford Jennings got a 93-yard (85-meter) kick return touchdown, and the Bengals took the lead.

Quarterback Joe Montana led the 49ers on a 92-yard (84-meter), game-winning drive.

MOST VALUABLE PLAYER:

JERRY RICE

Super Bowl XXV

January 27, 1991

NEW YORK GIANTS **20-19** **BUFFALO BILLS**

TAMPA STADIUM, TAMPA, FLORIDA

The Bills scored a field goal, a touchdown, and a safety. The Giants answered with two back-to-back touchdowns.

Down by two points in the fourth quarter, Giants kicker Matt Bahr made a 21-yard (19-meter), game-winning field goal.

This was the first of four Super Bowls that the Bills lost in a row from 1991 to 1994.

MOST VALUABLE PLAYER:

OTTIS ANDERSON

Super Bowl XLIII

February 1, 2009

PITTSBURGH STEELERS	27-23	ARIZONA CARDINALS

RAYMOND JAMES STADIUM, TAMPA, FLORIDA

The Steelers' amazing **defense** included safety Troy Polamalu and linebacker James Harrison.

Arizona came from behind to lead 23 to 20 with a little more than two minutes left in the game.

The Steelers drove down the field and won the game with a picture-perfect touchdown catch by wide receiver Santonio Holmes.

MOST VALUABLE PLAYER:

SANTONIO HOLMES

Super Bowl XLII

February 3, 2008

NEW YORK GIANTS	17-14	NEW ENGLAND PATRIOTS

UNIVERSITY OF PHOENIX STADIUM, GLENDALE, ARIZONA

After an 18-0 season, the New England Patriots hoped to be the second **undefeated** team in NFL history.

One of the greatest catches in Super Bowl history was made by Giants wide receiver David Tyree, who caught the ball on his helmet.

Down by four points with 35 seconds left in the game, Giants quarterback Eli Manning threw a 13-yard (12-meter) touchdown pass to wide receiver Plaxico Burress to earn the victory.

MOST VALUABLE PLAYER:

ELI MANNING

Super Bowl LII

February 4, 2018

PHILADELPHIA EAGLES **41-33** NEW ENGLAND PATRIOTS

U.S. BANK STADIUM, MINNEAPOLIS, MINNESOTA

Journeyman backup quarterback Nick Foles, along with a star defense, helped the Eagles win the NFC Championship to get to the Super Bowl.

The game is known for the "Philly Special," a trick play where tight end Trey Burton passed the ball to Nick Foles for a touchdown.

The Eagles pulled away in the fourth quarter and won with a touchdown by tight end Zach Ertz.

MOST VALUABLE PLAYER:

NICK FOLES

SUPER BOWL XLIX

February 1, 2015

NEW ENGLAND PATRIOTS **28-24** **SEATTLE SEAHAWKS**

UNIVERSITY OF PHOENIX STADIUM, GLENDALE, ARIZONA

In the fourth quarter, the Patriots were down by ten points. Then, they scored back-to-back touchdowns to take the lead.

With two minutes left in the game, Seahawks quarterback Russell Wilson led his team down the field.

On the two-yard line, Patriots cornerback Malcolm Butler intercepted a Seahawks pass, giving the Patriots the win.

MOST VALUABLE PLAYER:

TOM BRADY

Super Bowl LI

February 5, 2017

NEW ENGLAND PATRIOTS	34-28	ATLANTA FALCONS

NRG STADIUM, HOUSTON, TEXAS

In the third quarter, the Patriots were down 28 to 3. Then, the Patriots scored 25 straight points to tie the game.

In **overtime**, Patriots running back James White scored the winning touchdown.

This is the only Super Bowl to ever go into overtime.

MOST VALUABLE PLAYER:

TOM BRADY

GLOSSARY

defense (DEE-fens): the side that does not have the ball and that tries to stop the other team from scoring points

intercepted (in-tur-SEP-tid): stole the ball away from the other team

journeyman (JUR-nee-muhn): an experienced player who has played for many teams

offense (AW-fens): the side that has the ball and that tries to score points by moving the ball down the field

overtime (OH-vur-time): extra time added to a game because the score was tied at the end of normal play

turf (turf): the real or artificial grass that covers the playing field

undefeated (un-di-FEE-tuhd): not having any losses or defeats

underdogs (UHN-dur-dawgz): team that is expected to lose a game

INDEX

AFTER READING QUESTIONS

1. How do teams get to the Super Bowl?
2. What is the Super Bowl trophy called? Why?
3. Who won Super Bowl LI?
4. What journeyman quarterback helped the Eagles win Super Bowl LII?
5. What is the only Super Bowl to date to go into overtime?

About the Author

Ryan James lives in the western part of North Carolina with his dog Bailey. As a child, he would go to Carolina Panthers games with his dad while wearing the jersey of his favorite player, Steve Smith Sr. When he's not watching football, Ryan goes hiking and biking in the mountains near his house.

Written by: Ryan James
Cover Design by: Rhea Magaro-Wallace
Interior Design by: Kathy Walsh
Editor: Kim Thompson

Library of Congress PCN Data
Top Super Bowls / Ryan James
Top Sports Championships
ISBN 978-1-63897-482-6 (hard cover)
ISBN 978-1-63897-597-7 (paperback)
ISBN 978-1-63897-712-4 (EPUB)
ISBN 978-1-63897-827-5 (eBook)
Library of Congress Control Number: 2022933971

Printed in the United States of America.

Photographs/Shutterstock: Cover ©winui, ©Kevin Dietsch; Title Pg ©winui, ©EFKS; Pg 3 ©EFKS; Pg 4, 6, 8, 10, 12, 14, 16, 18, 20 ©Sedulur Grafis; Pg 7, 9, 11, 13, 15, 17, 19, 21 ©Little_ Monster_2070, Sakina Xalilova; Pg 5 ©Dylan Stewart; Pg 6 ©DAVID PURDY; Pg 8 ©John W. McDonough/Icon SMI; Pg 10 ©John Barrett; Pg 12 ©Scott A. Miller; Pg 14 ©Karl Mondon; Pg 16 ©Elizabeth Flores; Pg 18 ©KEVIN DIETSCH; Pg 20 ©Dave Clements/Sipa USA

Seahorse Publishing Company
www.seahorsepub.com

Published in the United States
Seahorse Publishing
PO Box 771325
Coral Springs, FL 33077

SEAHORSE PUBLISHING